The Stress Management Handbook: Tips and Strategies for Reducing Stress and Improving Overall Wellbeing

Onah Eje Johnbless

A practical guide to managing stress and achieving a better work-life balance.

Copyright

© 2024
Onah Eje Johnbless

Table of Contents

Part 2: Stress Management Techniques

Part 3: Lifestyle Changes for Stress Reduction

Preface

Welcome to The Stress Management Handbook, a comprehensive guide to understanding and managing stress. In today's fast-paced and often overwhelming world, stress has become an all-too-familiar companion for many of us. Whether you're struggling with anxiety, feeling overwhelmed by work or personal responsibilities, or simply seeking a greater sense of calm and well-being, this book is here to help.

As someone who has personally experienced the debilitating effects of stress, I know how it can impact every aspect of your life. But I also know that there is hope for a better tomorrow. With the right tools, strategies, and mindset, you can learn to manage stress and cultivate a more peaceful, productive, and fulfilling life.

This handbook is designed to provide you with a holistic approach to stress management, covering everything from the physical and emotional symptoms of stress to the practical tips and techniques for reducing stress and improving overall well-being. You'll learn how to:

- Identify and understand your personal stressors

- Develop effective coping mechanisms and stress-reducing habits
- Improve your physical and mental health
- Enhance your relationships and work-life balance
- Cultivate resilience and a growth mindset

Throughout these pages, you'll find a wealth of information, insights, and inspiration to support you on your journey towards a more stress-free and joyful life. Whether you're just starting out or seeking to deepen your understanding of stress management, this handbook is here to guide and empower you every step of the way.

So take a deep breath, relax, and let's get started on this transformative journey together!

Sincerely,

Onah Eje Johnbless

Introduction

Welcome to The Stress Management Handbook, a comprehensive and practical guide to understanding and managing stress. In today's fast-paced and increasingly demanding world, stress has become an all-too-familiar companion for many of us. Whether you're struggling with anxiety, feeling overwhelmed by work or personal responsibilities, or simply seeking a greater sense of calm and well-being, this book is here to help.

Stress is a natural and normal part of life, but chronic stress can have serious consequences on our physical and mental health, relationships, and overall quality of life. The good news is that stress is manageable, and with the right tools, strategies, and mindset, you can learn to reduce stress and cultivate a more peaceful, productive, and fulfilling life.

This handbook is designed to provide you with a holistic approach to stress management, covering everything from the physical and emotional symptoms of stress to the practical tips and techniques for reducing stress and improving overall well-being. You'll learn how to:

- Identify and understand your personal stressors
- Develop effective coping mechanisms and stress-reducing habits
- Improve your physical and mental health

- Enhance your relationships and work-life balance
- Cultivate resilience and a growth mindset

Throughout these pages, you'll find a wealth of information, insights, and inspiration to support you on your journey towards a more stress-free and joyful life. Whether you're just starting out or seeking to deepen your understanding of stress management, this handbook is here to guide and empower you every step of the way.

In the following chapters, we'll explore:

- The physical and emotional symptoms of stress
- The impact of stress on relationships and work-life balance
- Effective coping mechanisms and stress-reducing habits
- Practical tips for managing stress in the workplace and at home

- Strategies for cultivating resilience and a growth mindset
- The importance of self-care and self-compassion in stress management

By the end of this book, you'll have a comprehensive understanding of stress management and a toolkit of practical strategies to help you navigate life's challenges with greater ease, confidence, and joy.

So let's get started on this transformative journey together!

Part 1: Understanding Stress

Chapter 1:
What is Stress?

Stress is a complex and multifaceted concept that affects millions of people worldwide. It is a natural physical and mental response to a perceived threat or challenge, and it can have a significant impact on our overall health and wellbeing. In this chapter, we will explore the definition of stress, its history, and its effects on the body and mind.

Definition of Stress

Stress is defined as a state of mental or emotional strain or tension resulting from adverse or demanding circumstances. It is a normal response to a perceived threat or challenge, and it can be triggered by a wide range of factors, including work, relationships, finances, health, and major life changes.

History of Stress

The concept of stress has been around for centuries, but it wasn't until the 20th century that it became a widely recognized and studied phenomenon. The term "stress" was first coined by Hans Selye, a Hungarian-born endocrinologist, in the 1930s. Selye defined stress as "the non-specific response of the body to any demand placed upon it."

Physiological Response to Stress

When we perceive a threat or challenge, our body's "fight or flight" response is triggered, releasing stress hormones like adrenaline and cortisol into our system. These hormones prepare our body to either fight or flee by:

- Increasing heart rate and blood pressure
- Redirecting blood flow to muscles and vital organs
- Suppressing digestion and immune function
- Increasing glucose release for energy

This response was designed to be short-term, but in today's fast-paced world, our bodies are often in a state of prolonged stress, leading to negative effects on our physical and mental health.

Effects of Stress on the Body

Chronic stress can have serious physical health consequences, including:

  - Cardiovascular disease
  - Hypertension
  - Diabetes
  - Obesity
  - Gastrointestinal problems
  - Immune system suppression

Effects of Stress on the Mind

Stress can also have a significant impact on our mental health, leading to:

- Anxiety

- Depression
- Insomnia
- Memory and concentration problems
- Mood swings
- Irritability

Types of Stress

There are several types of stress, including:

- Acute stress: Short-term stress, such as meeting a deadline or preparing for an exam

- Chronic stress: Long-term stress, such as dealing with a chronic illness or difficult relationship

- Episodic stress: Repeated instances of acute stress, such as frequent deadlines or financial struggles

- Traumatic stress: Stress resulting from a traumatic event, such as a natural disaster or abuse

Stress is a natural response to a perceived threat or challenge, and it can have a significant impact on our physical and mental health. Understanding the definition, history, and effects of stress is crucial for developing effective stress management strategies. In the next chapter, we will explore the physical and mental effects of stress in more detail.

Chapter 2:
The Physical and Mental Effects of Stress

Stress can have a profound impact on both our physical and mental health. Chronic stress can lead to a range of physical health problems, including cardiovascular disease, digestive issues, and a weakened immune system. Additionally, stress can have a significant impact on our mental health, leading to anxiety, depression, and other mood disorders.

Physical Effects of Stress

1. **Cardiovascular Disease:** Stress can increase the risk of cardiovascular disease by raising blood pressure, heart rate, and cholesterol levels. For example, a person working long hours and experiencing chronic stress may be more likely to develop high blood pressure, which can lead to heart disease.

2. **Digestive Issues:** Stress can cause stomach problems, irritable bowel syndrome, and acid reflux. For instance, a

student experiencing stress during exam season may experience stomach cramps and diarrhea.

3. **Immune System Suppression:** Chronic stress can weaken the immune system, making us more susceptible to illness and infection. For example, a person experiencing chronic stress may be more likely to catch a cold or flu.

4. **Sleep Disturbances:** Stress can lead to insomnia, sleep deprivation, and other sleep-related problems. For instance, a person experiencing stress may lie awake at night, unable to fall asleep due to racing thoughts.

5. **Muscle Tension:** Stress can cause muscle tension, leading to headaches, back pain, and other musculoskeletal issues. For example, a person experiencing stress may clench their jaw, leading to tension headaches.

6. **Hormonal Imbalance:** Stress can disrupt hormonal balance, leading to issues such as thyroid problems and adrenal fatigue. For instance, a person experiencing chronic stress may develop hypothyroidism, a condition in which the thyroid gland doesn't produce enough hormones.

7. **Skin Problems:** Stress can trigger or exacerbate skin conditions such as acne, eczema, and psoriasis. For example, a person experiencing stress may experience a flare-up of acne or eczema.

Mental Effects of Stress

1. **Anxiety:** Stress can lead to anxiety, worry, and fear. For instance, a person experiencing stress may worry excessively about their finances or relationships.

2. **Depression:** Chronic stress can contribute to the development of

depression. For example, a person experiencing chronic stress may feel hopeless and disinterested in activities they once enjoyed.

3. **Mood Swings:** Stress can cause irritability, mood swings, and emotional reactivity. For instance, a person experiencing stress may snap at their partner or children.

4. **Memory and Concentration Problems:** Stress can impair memory, concentration, and cognitive function. For example, a person experiencing stress may have trouble focusing at work or remembering important tasks.

5. **Burnout:** Chronic stress can lead to emotional exhaustion, cynicism, and reduced performance. For instance, a person experiencing burnout may feel exhausted and disconnected from their work or relationships.

6. **Post-Traumatic Stress Disorder (PTSD):** Traumatic stress can lead to PTSD, a condition characterized by flashbacks, nightmares, and avoidance of triggers. For example, a person who experienced a traumatic event may develop PTSD and avoid places or situations that remind them of the event.

7. **Substance Abuse:** Stress can contribute to substance abuse and addiction. For instance, a person experiencing stress may turn to alcohol or drugs as a coping mechanism.

Stress can have a significant impact on both our physical and mental health. Understanding the physical and mental effects of stress is crucial for developing effective stress management strategies. By recognizing the signs and symptoms of stress, we can take steps to mitigate its negative effects and promote overall health and wellbeing. In the next chapter, we will explore the causes of stress and how to identify your stress triggers.

Chapter 3:
Identifying Your Stress Triggers

Identifying your stress triggers is a crucial step in managing stress. Stress triggers are the people, situations, or events that cause you to feel stressed. Once you know what your stress triggers are, you can develop strategies to avoid or cope with them.

Types of Stress Triggers

1. **Environmental Stress Triggers:** These are stressors in your physical environment, such as noise, pollution, or clutter.

2. **Social Stress Triggers:** These are stressors related to relationships, such as conflict, criticism, or social pressure.

3. **Psychological Stress Triggers:** These are stressors related to your thoughts and beliefs, such as perfectionism, self-doubt, or fear.

4. **Physiological Stress Triggers:** These are stressors related to your physical health, such as pain, fatigue, or illness.

Common Stress Triggers

1. Work-related stressors, such as deadlines, long hours, or difficult colleagues.

2. Financial stressors, such as debt, unemployment, or financial insecurity.

3. Relationship stressors, such as conflict, communication problems, or feeling trapped.

4. Health stressors, such as chronic illness, pain, or fear of illness.

5. Major life changes, such as moving, getting married, or having a child.

6. Traumatic events, such as abuse, neglect, or loss.

7. Social media, news, or other sources of constant stimulation.

Identifying Your Stress Triggers

1. **Keep a Stress Journal:** Write down when you feel stressed, what happened before and after, and how you felt.

2. **Reflect on Your Experiences:** Think about times when you felt stressed and what triggered it.

3. **Ask Yourself Questions:** What am I afraid of? What makes me feel anxious or overwhelmed?

4. **Seek Feedback:** Ask trusted friends, family, or a therapist what they think triggers your stress.

5. **Identify Patterns:** Look for common themes or patterns in your stress triggers.

Conclusion

Identifying your stress triggers is a crucial step in managing stress. By understanding what causes your stress, you can develop strategies to avoid or cope with those triggers. Remember, everyone's stress triggers are different, and it may take time and effort to identify yours. But with persistence and self-awareness, you can take the first step towards reducing your stress and improving your overall wellbeing.

In the next chapter, we will explore stress management techniques and strategies.

Part 2:
Stress Management Techniques

Chapter 4:
Deep Breathing and Relaxation Techniques

Deep breathing and relaxation techniques are powerful tools for managing stress and anxiety. These techniques can help calm the mind and body, reducing feelings of tension and overwhelm. In this chapter, we will explore the benefits of deep breathing and relaxation techniques, and provide guidance on how to incorporate them into your daily life.

__Benefits of Deep Breathing and Relaxation Techniques__

1. **Reduces Stress and Anxiety:** Deep breathing and relaxation techniques can help calm the mind and body, reducing feelings of stress and anxiety.

2. **Improves Sleep:** Practicing deep breathing and relaxation techniques before bed can improve sleep quality and duration.

3. **Boosts Mood:** Deep breathing and relaxation techniques can help reduce symptoms of depression and anxiety, leading to improved mood and overall wellbeing.

4. **Improves Focus and Concentration:** Deep breathing and relaxation techniques can help improve focus and concentration, leading to increased productivity and efficiency.

5. **Enhances Self-Awareness:** Deep breathing and relaxation techniques can help increase self-awareness, allowing individuals to better understand their thoughts, feelings, and behaviors.

Deep Breathing Techniques

1. **Diaphragmatic Breathing:** Also known as belly breathing, this technique involves breathing deeply into the diaphragm, rather than shallowly into the chest.

2. **4-7-8 Breathing:** This technique involves breathing in through the nose for a count of four, holding the breath for a count of seven, and exhaling through the mouth for a count of eight.

3. **Box Breathing:** This technique involves breathing in for a count of four, holding the breath for a count of four, exhaling for a

count of four, and holding the breath again for a count of four.

Relaxation Techniques

1. **Progressive Muscle Relaxation:** This technique involves tensing and relaxing different muscle groups in the body, starting with the toes and moving up to the head.

2. **Visualization:** This technique involves using the imagination to create a peaceful and relaxing scene, such as a beach or a forest.

3. **Mindfulness Meditation:** This technique involves focusing on the present moment, without judgment or distraction.

Tips for Incorporating Deep Breathing and Relaxation Techniques into Your Daily Life

1. **Start small:** Begin with short sessions (5-10 minutes) and gradually increase as you become more comfortable with the techniques.

2. **Find a quiet space:** Identify a quiet and comfortable space where you can practice deep breathing and relaxation techniques without distraction.

3. **Use reminders:** Set reminders on your phone or place a note in a visible location to remind you to practice deep breathing and relaxation techniques throughout the day.

4. **Make it a habit:** Incorporate deep breathing and relaxation techniques into your daily routine, such as right before bed or during your lunch break.

5. **Seek guidance:** Consider working with a therapist or coach who can provide guidance and support as you develop your deep breathing and relaxation techniques.

Deep breathing and relaxation techniques are powerful tools for managing stress and anxiety. By incorporating these techniques into your daily life, you can reduce feelings of tension and overwhelm, improve sleep and mood, and increase focus and concentration. Remember to start small, find a quiet space, use reminders, make it a habit, and seek guidance as needed. With consistent practice, you can develop a deeper sense of calm and wellbeing, leading to a happier and healthier life.

Chapter 5: Exercise and Physical Activity for Stress Relief

Exercise and physical activity are essential for overall health and wellbeing, and they can also play a crucial role in stress relief. Regular exercise can help reduce stress and anxiety by releasing endorphins, also known as "feel-good" hormones, which can improve mood and reduce tension. In this chapter, we will explore the benefits of exercise and physical activity for stress relief, and provide guidance on how to incorporate them into your daily life.

Benefits of Exercise and Physical Activity for Stress Relief

1. Reduces Stress and Anxiety: Exercise and physical activity can help reduce stress and anxiety by releasing endorphins, which can improve mood and reduce tension.

2. Improves Mood: Regular exercise can improve mood and reduce symptoms of depression and anxiety.

3. Enhances Sleep: Exercise and physical activity can help improve sleep quality and duration.

4. Boosts Energy: Regular exercise can increase energy levels and reduce fatigue.

5. Increases Self-Esteem: Exercise and physical activity can improve self-esteem and body image.

6. Reduces Muscle Tension: Exercise and physical activity can help reduce muscle tension and improve overall physical health.

Types of Exercise and Physical Activity for Stress Relief

1. Aerobic Exercise: Activities such as walking, running, swimming, and cycling can help reduce stress and anxiety.

2. Yoga and Pilates: These low-impact exercises can help improve flexibility, balance, and strength, while also reducing stress and anxiety.

3. Strength Training: Building muscle through strength training can help improve self-esteem and reduce stress and anxiety.

4. Mind-Body Exercise: Activities such as tai chi and qigong can help reduce stress and anxiety by promoting relaxation and improving mood.

5. Outdoor Activities: Spending time in nature through activities such as hiking, gardening, and outdoor sports can help reduce stress and anxiety.

Tips for Incorporating Exercise and Physical Activity into Your Daily Life

1. Start small: Begin with short sessions (20-30 minutes) and gradually increase as you become more comfortable.

2. Find an activity you enjoy: Engage in physical activities that bring you joy and make you feel good.

3. Schedule it in: Make exercise and physical activity a priority by scheduling it into your daily routine.

4. Find a workout buddy: Having a workout buddy can help keep you motivated and accountable.

5. Mix it up: Vary your exercise and physical activity routine to avoid boredom and prevent plateaus.

Examples:

Sarah starts her day with a 30-minute walk in the park to reduce stress and improve her mood.

Exercise and physical activity are essential for overall health and wellbeing, and they can also play a crucial role in stress relief. By incorporating exercise and physical activity into your daily life, you can reduce stress and anxiety, improve mood, enhance sleep, boost energy, increase self-esteem, and reduce muscle tension. Remember to start small, find an activity you enjoy, schedule it in, find a workout buddy, and mix it up to avoid boredom and prevent plateaus. With consistent exercise and physical activity, you can improve your overall health and wellbeing, and reduce stress and anxiety in your life.

Chapter 6:
Mindfulness and Meditation for Stress Reduction

Mindfulness and meditation are powerful tools for reducing stress and anxiety. These practices have been used for centuries to promote relaxation, calmness, and inner peace. In this chapter, we will explore the benefits of mindfulness and meditation for stress reduction, and provide guidance on how to incorporate them into your daily life.

What is Mindfulness and Meditation?

Mindfulness and meditation are practices that help you cultivate awareness, calmness, and clarity in your daily life. Here's a brief overview:

Mindfulness:

Mindfulness is the practice of being present in the moment, paying attention to your thoughts, feelings, and sensations without judgment.

   - It involves cultivating awareness of your experiences, thoughts, and emotions in a non-judgmental way.

   - Mindfulness helps you develop a greater sense of self-awareness, allowing you to respond to situations more skillfully and make better choices.

Meditation:

Meditation is a practice that involves training your mind to focus, relax, and become more aware.

   - It often involves sitting comfortably, closing your eyes, and focusing on a specific object, thought, or activity (like breathing or a mantra).

   - Meditation helps calm the mind, reduce stress and anxiety, and increase feelings of calmness, clarity, and inner peace.

By combining mindfulness and meditation, you can:

- Reduce stress and anxiety
- Improve sleep
- Boost mood and emotional well-being
- Enhance focus and concentration
- Increase self-awareness and self-acceptance
- Develop a greater sense of calmness and inner peace

Remember, mindfulness and meditation are practices that take time and patience to develop. Start small, be consistent, and be gentle with yourself as you explore these powerful tools for cultivating a more mindful and compassionate life.

Benefits of Mindfulness and Meditation for Stress Reduction

1. **Reduces Stress and Anxiety:**
Mindfulness and meditation have been shown to reduce stress and anxiety by promoting relaxation and calmness.

2. **Improves Sleep:** Regular mindfulness and meditation practice can improve sleep quality and duration.

3. **Boosts Mood:** Mindfulness and meditation can increase feelings of happiness and well-being, reducing symptoms of depression and anxiety.

4. **Improves Focus and Concentration:** Mindfulness and meditation can improve focus and concentration, leading to increased productivity and efficiency.

5. **Enhances Self-Awareness:** Mindfulness and meditation can increase self-awareness, allowing individuals to better understand their thoughts, feelings, and behaviors.

6. **Lowers Blood Pressure:** Regular mindfulness and meditation practice can lower blood pressure and reduce the risk of heart disease.

7. **Improves Relationships:** Mindfulness and meditation can improve relationships by increasing empathy, communication, and understanding.

Types of Mindfulness and Meditation Practices

1. **Mindful Breathing**: Focusing on the breath to promote relaxation and calmness.

2. **Body Scan Meditation:** Bringing awareness to the body to release tension and promote relaxation.

3. **Loving-Kindness Meditation:** Focusing on sending kindness and compassion to oneself and others.

4. **Guided Meditation:** Following a guided audio or video to lead the meditation practice.

5. **Transcendental Meditation:** Using a mantra to quiet the mind and promote inner peace.

Tips for Incorporating Mindfulness and Meditation into Your Daily Life

1. Start small: Begin with short sessions (5-10 minutes) and gradually increase as you become more comfortable.

2. **Find a quiet space:** Identify a quiet and comfortable space where you can practice mindfulness and meditation without distraction.

3. **Use reminders:** Set reminders on your phone or place a note in a visible location to

remind you to practice mindfulness and meditation.

4. **Make it a habit:** Incorporate mindfulness and meditation into your daily routine, such as right before bed or during your lunch break.

5. **Seek guidance:** Consider working with a therapist or coach who can provide guidance and support as you develop your mindfulness and meditation practice.

Mindfulness and meditation are powerful tools for reducing stress and anxiety. By incorporating these practices into your daily life, you can reduce stress and anxiety, improve sleep, boost mood, improve focus and concentration, enhance self-awareness, lower blood pressure, and improve relationships. Remember to start small, find a quiet space, use reminders, make it a habit, and seek guidance as needed. With consistent practice, you can experience the many benefits of mindfulness and meditation for stress reduction.

Chapter 7:
Time Management and Prioritization Strategies

Effective time management and prioritization are essential skills for reducing stress and achieving goals. When you manage your time well, you can accomplish more in less time, reduce feelings of overwhelm, and enjoy a better work-life balance. In this chapter, we will explore time management and prioritization strategies to help you make the most of your time.

Time management and prioritization are skills and strategies used to optimize the use of time and energy to achieve goals and objectives. Effective time management and prioritization enable individuals to:

1. Set clear goals and objectives
2. Identify and prioritize tasks based on importance and urgency
3. Allocate time and resources efficiently
4. Minimize distractions and interruptions
5. Maximize productivity and efficiency
6. Reduce stress and feeling of overwhelm
7. Improve work-life balance
8. Enhance overall performance and achievement

Time management involves:

- Planning and scheduling
- Organizing tasks and activities
- Setting deadlines and timelines
- Managing distractions and interruptions
- Using tools like calendars, to-do lists, and timers

Prioritization involves:

- Identifying and categorizing tasks based on importance and urgency
- Focusing on high-priority tasks first
- Allocating time and resources accordingly
- Eliminating or delegating non-essential tasks
- Regularly reviewing and adjusting priorities as needed

Time Management Strategies:

1. **Set Clear Goals:** Establishing clear goals helps you focus on what needs to be accomplished and allocate your time accordingly.

2. **Use a Planner or Calendar:** Write down all your tasks, appointments, and deadlines in a planner or calendar to keep track of your schedule.

3. **Prioritize Tasks:** Identify the most important and urgent tasks and tackle them first.

4. **Break Tasks into Smaller Chunks**: Divide large tasks into smaller, manageable chunks to avoid feeling overwhelmed.

5. **Avoid Multitasking:** Focus on one task at a time to ensure efficiency and quality.

6. **Take Regular Breaks:** Take short breaks to recharge and avoid burnout.

7. **Learn to Say No:** Set boundaries and learn to say no to non-essential tasks that can derail your schedule.

8. **Eliminate Distractions:** Minimize distractions such as social media, email, or phone notifications to stay focused.

9. **Delegate Tasks:** Assign tasks to others when possible to free up time for more important tasks.

10. **Review and Adjust:** Regularly review your time management strategy and make adjustments as needed.

Prioritization Strategies:

1. **Eisenhower Matrix:** Use the Eisenhower Matrix to categorize tasks into urgent vs. important and focus on the most critical ones.

2. **ABCD Method:** Label tasks as A (high priority), B (medium priority), C (low priority), or D (deadline not set) to prioritize accordingly.

3. **Must-Should-Could-Won't (MSCW):** Categorize tasks into must-do, should-do, could-do, and won't-do to prioritize and eliminate non-essential tasks.

4. **Priority Matrix:** Use a priority matrix to evaluate tasks based on their impact and urgency.

5. **Focus on High-Impact Tasks:** Identify tasks that have the greatest impact and prioritize them first.

By implementing these time management and prioritization strategies, you can optimize your productivity, reduce stress, and achieve your goals. Remember to regularly review and adjust your approach to ensure it continues to work for you.

Combining effective time management and prioritization, individuals can optimize their productivity, achieve their goals, and enjoy a better work-life balance.

Chapter 8: Communication Skills for Managing Stress

Effective communication is a vital skill for managing stress and achieving overall well-being. When we communicate effectively, we can express our needs, feelings, and concerns in a clear and assertive manner, which helps to reduce stress and anxiety. In this chapter, we will explore the importance of communication skills for managing stress and provide practical tips and strategies for improving communication.

What are Communication Skills?

Communication skills are the abilities and techniques used to convey information, ideas, and messages effectively to others. These skills enable individuals to interact and connect with others, build relationships, and achieve personal and professional goals.

Communication skills are essential in various aspects of life, including:

- Personal relationships
- Professional settings (work, business, etc.)
- Education
- Public speaking
- Conflict resolution
- Teamwork and collaboration
- Leadership
- Customer service

Developing strong communication skills can help individuals:

- Build strong relationships
- Achieve personal and professional goals
- Resolve conflicts effectively
- Communicate ideas and messages clearly
- Understand and empathize with others

- Succeed in their careers and personal lives.

Why Communication Skills are Essential for Managing Stress

1. **Expressing Emotions:** Communication helps us express our emotions and feelings, which is essential for managing stress.

2. **Building Relationships:** Good communication skills help build strong relationships, which are crucial for emotional support and stress management.

3. **Resolving Conflicts:** Effective communication helps resolve conflicts and misunderstandings, reducing stress and tension.

4. **Setting Boundaries:** Communication skills enable us to set clear boundaries, prioritizing self-care and stress reduction.

5. **Seeking Help:** Good communication skills allow us to seek help and support when needed, reducing feelings of isolation and stress.

Practical Communication Tips for Managing Stress

1. **Active Listening:** Pay attention to others, focus on the conversation, and ask clarifying questions.

2. **Assertive Expression:** Express your needs, feelings, and concerns in a clear and respectful manner.

3. **Non-Verbal Communication:** Use positive body language, tone, and facial expressions to convey confidence and calmness.

4. **Empathy and Understanding:** Show compassion and understanding towards

others, acknowledging their feelings and perspectives.

5. **Clarify Expectations:** Clearly communicate expectations, roles, and responsibilities to avoid misunderstandings and stress.

6. **Use "I" Statements:** Instead of blaming others, use "I" statements to express feelings and thoughts.

7. **Avoid Assumptions:** Don't assume others' thoughts or feelings; ask open-ended questions to clarify.

8. **Practice Mindfulness:** Be present and mindful in conversations, focusing on the moment.

9. **Seek Feedback:** Encourage constructive feedback to improve communication and relationships.

10. **Be Open-Minded:** Be receptive to different perspectives and opinions, fostering a supportive environment.

By incorporating these communication skills into your daily life, you can effectively manage stress, build strong relationships, and achieve overall well-being. Remember, communication is a skill that can be developed with practice, patience, and persistence.

Part 3:
Lifestyle Changes for Stress Reduction

Chapter 9:
Healthy Eating Habits for Stress Management

Healthy eating habits play a crucial role in managing stress and anxiety. A well-nourished body and mind are better equipped to handle the challenges of stress, and a healthy diet can help mitigate its negative effects. In this chapter, we will explore the importance of healthy eating habits for stress management, discuss the best foods for stress reduction, and provide practical tips for incorporating healthy eating habits into your lifestyle.

The Impact of Stress on Eating Habits

Stress can significantly impact our eating habits, leading to:

1. **Emotional Eating:** Using food as a coping mechanism for stress and emotions.

2. **Poor Food Choices:** Opting for comfort foods or convenience foods high in sugar, salt, and unhealthy fats.

3. **Irregular Eating:** Skipping meals or eating at irregular times, leading to energy crashes and mood swings.

4. **Digestive Issues:** Stress can exacerbate digestive problems like bloating, cramps, and irritable bowel syndrome (IBS).

Best Foods for Stress Reduction

1. **Omega-3 Rich Foods:** Fatty fish (salmon, sardines), nuts (walnuts, almonds), and seeds (chia, flax) support brain health and reduce inflammation.

2. **Complex Carbohydrates:** Whole grains (brown rice, quinoa), fruits (berries, apples), and vegetables (leafy greens, bell peppers) provide sustained energy and fiber.

3. **Protein-Rich Foods:** Lean meats (chicken, turkey), legumes (lentils,

chickpeas), and dairy (yogurt, milk) support mood regulation and satiety.

4. **Healthy Fats:** Avocados, olive oil, and nuts provide sustained energy and support brain function.

5. **Fermented Foods:** Yogurt, kimchi, and sauerkraut contain probiotics, supporting gut health and immune function.

6. **B Vitamins:** Foods rich in B vitamins (leafy greens, beans, whole grains) support energy production and mood regulation.

7. **Magnesium-Rich Foods:** Dark chocolate, spinach, and almonds help regulate stress hormones and promote relaxation.

Practical Tips for Healthy Eating Habits

1. **Meal Planning:** Plan meals in advance to ensure healthy choices and reduce stress.

2. **Grocery Shopping:** Focus on whole, unprocessed foods and avoid sugary snacks.

3. **Mindful Eating:** Eat slowly, savoring each bite, and pay attention to hunger and fullness cues.

4. **Hydration:** Drink plenty of water throughout the day, aiming for at least eight glasses.

5. **Regular Meals:** Eat regular, balanced meals to maintain energy and mood stability.

6. **Healthy Snacking:** Choose nuts, fruits, and veggies as snacks to curb cravings and support energy.

7. **Cooking at Home:** Prepare meals at home using fresh ingredients to control nutrient content and portion sizes.

8. **Reducing Caffeine and Sugar:** Limit or avoid sugary drinks and caffeine to minimize energy crashes and mood swings.

9. **Seeking Support:** Consult a registered dietitian or nutritionist for personalized guidance on healthy eating habits.

By incorporating these healthy eating habits into your lifestyle, you can effectively manage stress and anxiety, improving your overall well-being and resilience. Remember, a balanced diet is just one aspect of a comprehensive stress management plan, and combining healthy eating habits with other stress-reducing techniques will yield the best results.

Chapter 10:

Sleep and Relaxation Techniques for Stress Relief

Sleep and relaxation are essential components of a healthy stress management plan. During sleep, our bodies repair and rejuvenate themselves, while relaxation techniques help calm the mind and body, reducing stress and anxiety. In this chapter, we will explore the importance of sleep and relaxation for stress relief, discuss various relaxation techniques, and provide practical tips for improving sleep quality.

The Importance of Sleep for Stress Relief

1. **Physical Restoration:** Sleep helps repair and regenerate damaged cells, build bone and muscle, and strengthen the immune system.

2. **Mental Rejuvenation:** Sleep helps clear mental fog, improve concentration, and enhance problem-solving skills.

3. **Emotional Regulation:** Sleep helps regulate emotions, reducing stress, anxiety, and depression.

4. **Hormone Regulation:** Sleep helps regulate hormones, including stress hormones like cortisol and adrenaline.

Relaxation Techniques for Stress Relief

1. **Deep Breathing Exercises:** Slow, deliberate breathing helps calm the mind and body.

2. **Progressive Muscle Relaxation:** Tensing and relaxing muscles helps release physical tension.

3. **Mindfulness Meditation:** Focusing on the present moment reduces worries and stress.

4. **Visualization:** Imagining a peaceful scene or scenario helps calm the mind.

5. **Yoga:** Combining physical postures, breathing techniques, and meditation reduces stress and anxiety.

6. **Tai Chi:** Slow, flowing movements promote relaxation and balance.

7. **Massage Therapy:** Physical touch reduces muscle tension and promotes relaxation.

8. **Aromatherapy:** Certain scents like lavender and vanilla promote relaxation and calmness.

9. **Listening to Music:** Calming music reduces stress and anxiety.

10. **Nature Therapy:** Spending time in nature promotes relaxation and reduces stress.

Practical Tips for Improving Sleep Quality

1. **Establish a Bedtime Routine:** Develop a calming pre-sleep routine to signal the body for sleep.

2. **Create a Sleep-Conducive Environment:** Make the bedroom a sleep sanctuary with a comfortable bed, dark curtains, and quiet atmosphere.

3. **Stick to a Sleep Schedule:** Go to bed and wake up at consistent times, including weekends.

4. **Avoid Stimulants Before Bedtime:** Avoid caffeine, nicotine, and electronic screens for at least an hour before bed.

5. **Limit Naps:** Keep naps short (under 30 minutes) and avoid napping close to bedtime.

6. **Exercise Regularly**: Regular physical activity promotes better sleep, but avoid vigorous exercise before bedtime.

7. **Manage Stress:** Engage in stress-reducing activities, like relaxation techniques, to clear your mind before bed.

8. **Avoid Heavy Meals Before Bedtime:** Finish eating at least 2-3 hours before bed to avoid discomfort and indigestion.

9. **Get Morning Sunlight:** Exposure to natural light in the morning helps regulate the circadian rhythms.

10. **Consider Professional Help:** If sleep problems persist, consult a healthcare professional or sleep specialist.

Implementing these sleep and relaxation techniques into your daily routine, you can effectively manage stress and anxiety, improving your overall well-being and resilience. Remember, a comprehensive stress management plan includes a combination of healthy habits, including sleep, relaxation, exercise, and healthy eating.

Chapter 11:
Leisure Activities and Hobbies for Stress Reduction

Engaging in leisure activities and hobbies is an excellent way to reduce stress and improve overall well-being. These activities provide a healthy distraction from the pressures of daily life, allowing individuals to relax, unwind, and recharge. In this chapter, we will explore the benefits of leisure activities and hobbies for stress reduction, discuss various types of activities, and provide tips for incorporating them into your lifestyle.

Benefits of Leisure Activities and Hobbies for Stress Reduction

1. **Reduces Stress and Anxiety:** Engaging in enjoyable activities helps reduce stress hormones like cortisol and adrenaline.

2. **Improves Mood:** Leisure activities release endorphins, also known as "feel-good" hormones, which improve mood and reduce symptoms of depression.

3. **Enhances Creativity:** Engaging in creative activities like art, music, or writing stimulates the mind and fosters creativity.

4. **Fosters Social Connections:** Joining clubs or groups related to your hobby helps build social connections and a sense of community.

5. **Improves Cognitive Function:** Engaging in mentally stimulating activities like puzzles, games, or learning a new skill improves cognitive function and reduces the risk of cognitive decline.

6. **Boosts Self-Esteem:** Developing skills and expertise in a hobby enhances self-esteem and confidence.

7. **Provides Relaxation and Calm:** Leisure activities like reading, listening to music, or taking a relaxing bath help calm the mind and body.

Definition of Leisure Activity and Hobby

Leisure activity and hobby are often used interchangeably, but they have slightly different meanings:

Leisure activity:
A leisure activity is something you do in your free time, outside of work or daily responsibilities, to relax, enjoy yourself, and recharge. It can be a casual, informal activity that brings you pleasure and helps you unwind. Examples of leisure activities include:

- Reading
- Watching TV or movies
- Taking a walk or hike
- Listening to music
- Playing video games
- Browsing social media

Hobby:
A hobby, on the other hand, is a more structured and often creative activity that you pursue regularly, with a sense of

purpose and dedication. Hobbies often require some level of skill or expertise and can be a source of personal fulfillment and achievement. Examples of hobbies include:

- Painting or drawing
- Playing a musical instrument
- Gardening
- Cooking or baking
- Writing (fiction, nonfiction, or journalism)
- Photography
- Crafting (knitting, sewing, woodworking, etc.)
- Sports or fitness activities (playing on a team, training for a marathon, etc.)

Key differences:

- Leisure activities are often more passive and relaxing, while hobbies are more active and engaging.
- Leisure activities may be done sporadically, while hobbies are often

pursued regularly and with a sense of commitment.
- Leisure activities may not require much skill or expertise, while hobbies often do.

It's worth noting that the distinction between leisure activities and hobbies can be blurry, and many activities can fall into both categories depending on how you approach them. For example, playing guitar can be a leisure activity if you play casually for fun, but it can also be a hobby if you practice regularly and strive to improve your skills.

Types of Leisure Activities and Hobbies

1. **Creative Pursuits:** Art, music, writing, crafting, and other creative activities.

2. **Sports and Fitness:** Team sports, individual sports, fitness classes, or outdoor activities like hiking or cycling.

3. **Games and Puzzles:** Board games, card games, video games, crosswords, or other mentally stimulating activities.

4. **Outdoor Activities:** Gardening, camping, fishing, or simply spending time in nature.

5. **Social Activities**: Joining clubs, volunteering, or participating in group events.

6. **Relaxation Techniques:** Meditation, yoga, or other activities promoting relaxation and calm.

7. **Learning and Personal Growth:** Taking classes, workshops, or online courses to develop new skills or knowledge.

Tips for Incorporating Leisure Activities and Hobbies into Your Lifestyle

1. **Schedule Time:** Set aside time each week for your hobby or leisure activity.

2. **Explore New Activities:** Try new things to find what brings you joy and relaxation.

3. **Join a Community:** Connect with others who share your interests.

4. **Start Small:** Begin with short, manageable sessions and gradually increase time and intensity.

5. **Make it Convenient:** Find activities that can be done at home or in your free time.

6. **Prioritize Self-Care:** Remember that leisure activities are essential for stress reduction and overall well-being.

7. **Be Patient:** Developing a new hobby or activity takes time, so be patient and enjoy the process.

Incorporating leisure activities and hobbies into your lifestyle can have a significant impact on stress reduction and overall well-being. By exploring various activities and finding what brings you joy and relaxation, you can improve your mental and physical health, enhance your creativity and cognitive function, and foster social connections and a sense of community. Remember to prioritize self-care and make time for these essential activities.

Chapter 12:
Building a Support Network for Stress Management

Having a strong support network is crucial for effective stress management. A support network consists of individuals who provide emotional, practical, and informational support, helping you navigate stressful situations and maintain overall well-being. In this chapter, we will explore the importance of building a support network, discuss various types of support networks, and provide tips for creating and maintaining a robust support system.

What is Support Networks?

A support network refers to a group of individuals who provide emotional, practical, and informational support to help a person cope with challenges, stress, and difficult situations. These networks can be formal or informal and consist of:

1. Family members
2. Friends
3. Colleagues
4. Neighbors
5. Social groups
6. Online communities
7. Professional counselors or therapists

8. Support groups (e.g., 12-step programs)
9. Mentors or coaches
10. Community organizations

A support network offers various types of support, including:

1. Emotional support: Listening, empathy, encouragement, and validation.
2. Practical support: Help with tasks, errands, or daily responsibilities.
3. Informational support: Guidance, advice, and resources.
4. Financial support: Assistance with financial needs or expenses.
5. Social support: Companionship, social interaction, and a sense of belonging.

Having a strong support network can help individuals:

1. Manage stress and anxiety
2. Cope with trauma or difficult experiences
3. Build resilience and self-esteem

4. Improve mental and physical health
5. Navigate significant life changes or transitions
6. Enhance overall well-being and quality of life

Support networks can be tailored to specific needs and circumstances, and they can evolve over time as individuals face new challenges or experiences.

Importance of Building a Support Network

1. **Emotional Support:** A support network offers emotional support, reducing feelings of loneliness and isolation.

2. **Practical Help:** Network members can provide practical assistance, such as errands, household chores, or childcare.

3. **Informational Support:** A support network can offer valuable advice, resources, and guidance.

4. **Stress Reduction:** Having a support network helps reduce stress by sharing burdens and providing encouragement.

5. **Improved Mental Health:** A strong support network is linked to better mental health outcomes, including reduced symptoms of depression and anxiety.

Types of Support Networks

1. **Family Support:** Immediate and extended family members can provide emotional and practical support.

2. **Friend Support:** Close friends offer emotional support, companionship, and practical help.

3. **Peer Support:** Colleagues, classmates, or social group members can provide emotional support and understanding.

4. **Professional Support:** Mental health professionals, coaches, or mentors offer guidance and support.

5. **Online Support:** Online communities, forums, and social media groups provide access to a wider support network.

Tips for Creating and Maintaining a Support Network

1. **Identify Supportive Individuals:** Recognize people in your life who offer emotional support and encouragement.

2. **Nurture Relationships:** Invest time and effort in building and maintaining relationships with supportive individuals.

3. **Join Social Groups:** Engage in social activities, clubs, or organizations to expand your support network.

4. **Seek Professional Help:** Consult with mental health professionals or coaches for guidance and support.

5. **Be Open and Honest:** Share your feelings, concerns, and needs with your support network.

6. **Reciprocate Support:** Offer support to others in your network, fostering a sense of mutual support.

7. **Prioritize Self-Care:** Take care of your physical, emotional, and mental well-being to maintain a strong support network.

8. **Be Patient and Persistent:** Building a support network takes time, effort, and perseverance.

By investing in a support network, you can develop a robust system of emotional, practical, and informational support, helping you manage stress and maintain overall well-being. Remember to nurture your relationships, seek help when needed, and prioritize self-care to ensure a strong and supportive network.

Part 4:
Managing Stress in Specific Situations

Chapter 13:
Managing Stress at Work

The modern workplace can be a significant source of stress, with demanding deadlines, heavy workloads, and high expectations. Chronic stress can lead to burnout, decreased productivity, and a range of physical and mental health problems. In this chapter, we will explore the causes of workplace stress, discuss its impact on individuals and organizations, and provide practical strategies for managing stress at work.

Causes of Workplace Stress

1. Excessive workload and long hours
2. Lack of control and autonomy
3. Poor communication and unclear expectations
4. Conflicting priorities and deadlines
5. Unsupportive work environment and culture
6. Bullying, harassment, and discrimination
7. Fear of job insecurity and layoffs
8. Lack of recognition and rewards

9. Poor work-life balance
10. Technological stress and digital overload

Impact of Workplace Stress

1. Decreased productivity and performance
2. Increased absenteeism and turnover
3. Mental health problems (anxiety, depression, burnout)
4. Physical health problems (headaches, back pain, cardiovascular disease)
5. Strained relationships with colleagues and management
6. Decreased job satisfaction and engagement
7. Negative impact on personal life and relationships

Strategies for Managing Stress at Work

1. Prioritize tasks and focus on high-priority tasks
2. Set realistic goals and deadlines

3. Take regular breaks and practice self-care
4. Communicate effectively with colleagues and management
5. Seek support from HR, employee assistance programs, or mental health professionals
6. Develop a growth mindset and focus on learning and development
7. Establish clear boundaries and prioritize work-life balance
8. Engage in stress-reducing activities (meditation, yoga, exercise)
9. Seek feedback and recognition
10. Consider flexible work arrangements (telecommuting, flexible hours)

Organizational Strategies for Managing Stress

1. Foster an open and supportive work culture
2. Encourage work-life balance and flexible work arrangements

3. Provide employee assistance programs and mental health resources
4. Offer training and development opportunities
5. Recognize and reward employees' contributions
6. Conduct regular employee feedback and engagement surveys
7. Implement stress-reducing initiatives (wellness programs, mindfulness training)
8. Encourage teamwork and collaboration
9. Provide resources for managing workload and prioritizing tasks
10. Lead by example and prioritize employee well-being

By understanding the causes of workplace stress and implementing effective strategies for managing stress, individuals and organizations can promote a healthier, more productive, and more supportive work environment. Remember, managing stress at work is an ongoing process that requires effort, commitment, and a willingness to prioritize well-being.

Chapter 14: Managing Stress in Relationships

Relationships are a vital aspect of our lives, providing emotional support, companionship, and a sense of belonging. However, relationships can also be a significant source of stress, particularly when conflicts arise, communication breaks down, or expectations are unmet. In this chapter, we will explore the impact of stress on relationships, discuss common sources of relationship stress, and provide practical strategies for managing stress in relationships.

Impact of Stress on Relationships

1. Communication breakdown
2. Increased conflict
3. Emotional distancing
4. Decreased intimacy
5. Increased resentment
6. Decreased empathy
7. Increased defensiveness
8. Decreased problem-solving
9. Increased feelings of hopelessness
10. Decreased relationship satisfaction

Common Sources of Relationship Stress

1. Financial disagreements
2. Communication problems
3. Infidelity
4. Parenting disagreements
5. In-laws and extended family conflicts
6. Power struggles
7. Intimacy issues
8. Different goals and values

9. Lack of quality time together
10. Unresolved conflicts

Strategies for Managing Stress in Relationships

1. Practice active listening and empathy
2. Use effective communication skills (e.g., "I" statements, non-judgmental language)
3. Address conflicts promptly and constructively
4. Show appreciation and gratitude
5. Schedule quality time together
6. Practice forgiveness and letting go
7. Seek outside help (counseling, therapy)
8. Develop a growth mindset and work on personal growth
9. Establish boundaries and prioritize self-care
10. Cultivate a sense of humor and playfulness

Effective Communication in Relationships

1. Use "I" statements instead of "you"
statements
2. Practice active listening and empathy
3. Avoid blaming and criticizing
4. Use non-judgmental language
5. Avoid assumptions and clarifying
expectations
6. Show appreciation and gratitude
7. Use positive language and reinforcement
8. Be open and honest
9. Avoid interrupting and dismissing
10. Practice mindfulness and presence in
conversations

Conflict Resolution in Relationships

1. Address conflicts promptly
2. Use effective communication skills
3. Listen to each other's perspectives
4. Avoid blaming and criticizing
5. Focus on finding solutions
6. Seek outside help if necessary
7. Practice forgiveness and letting go

8. Show empathy and understanding
9. Be willing to compromise
10. Follow up and evaluate progress

By understanding the impact of stress on relationships and implementing effective strategies for managing stress, individuals can cultivate healthier, more fulfilling relationships. Remember, relationships involve effort and commitment from both parties, and managing stress in relationships is an ongoing process that requires patience, empathy, and effective communication.

Chapter 15:
Managing Stress during Major Life Changes

Major life changes can be incredibly stressful, whether they are positive or negative. Events like moving, getting married, having a child, or experiencing the loss of a loved one can cause significant emotional upheaval. In this chapter, we will explore the impact of major life changes on stress levels, discuss common major life changes that cause stress, and provide practical strategies for managing stress during these times.

Impact of Major Life Changes on Stress Levels

1. Emotional overload
2. Increased anxiety
3. Decreased sense of control
4. Changes in routine and structure
5. Fear of the unknown
6. Overwhelming responsibilities
7. Financial stress
8. Social support changes
9. Identity changes
10. Grief and loss

Common Major Life Changes that Cause Stress

1. Moving or relocating
2. Getting married or divorced
3. Having a child or becoming a parent
4. Experiencing the loss of a loved one
5. Changing jobs or careers
6. Health crises or chronic illness
7. Financial difficulties or debt
8. Education or academic changes
9. Relationship changes or breakups
10. Natural disasters or traumatic events

Strategies for Managing Stress during Major Life Changes

1. Practice self-care and prioritize well-being
2. Seek social support from loved ones or professionals
3. Take breaks and engage in relaxation techniques
4. Reframe negative thoughts and focus on positivity

5. Set realistic goals and expectations
6. Stay organized and manage time effectively
7. Seek professional help when needed
8. Engage in activities that bring joy and fulfillment
9. Practice mindfulness and presence
10. Develop a growth mindset and focus on personal growth

Additional Tips for Managing Stress during Major Life Changes

1. Allow yourself to feel emotions and process them
2. Take care of physical health and well-being
3. Set boundaries and prioritize self-care
4. Practice gratitude and appreciation
5. Seek out new experiences and opportunities
6. Focus on the present moment and what can be controlled

7. Develop a support network and community
8. Engage in activities that promote relaxation and stress reduction
9. Practice self-compassion and self-forgiveness
10. Celebrate milestones and accomplishments

Understanding the impact of major life changes on stress levels and implementing effective strategies for managing stress, individuals can navigate these significant events with greater ease and resilience. Remember, major life changes are a natural part of life, and with the right mindset and tools, individuals can thrive during these times.

Chapter 16:

Managing Stress during Traumatic Events

Traumatic events can have a profound impact on an individual's mental and emotional well-being, causing significant stress and potentially leading to long-term effects such as post-traumatic stress disorder (PTSD). In this chapter, we will explore the impact of traumatic events on stress levels, discuss common traumatic events that cause stress, and provide practical strategies for managing stress during and after these events.

Impact of Traumatic Events on Stress Levels

1. Acute stress response
2. Hyperarousal and hypervigilance
3. Dissociation and numbing
4. Intrusive memories and flashbacks
5. Avoidance of triggers and reminders

6. Emotional dysregulation
7. Social withdrawal and isolation
8. Physical symptoms and health problems
9. Cognitive impairment and memory issues
10. Spiritual and existential crises

Common Traumatic Events that Cause Stress

1. Natural disasters (e.g., hurricanes, earthquakes)
2. Sexual assault and abuse
3. Physical assault and violence
4. War and combat
5. Accidents and injuries
6. Loss of a loved one or grief
7. Terrorism and mass violence
8. Displacement and refugee experiences
9. Medical trauma (e.g., illness, surgery)
10. Psychological trauma (e.g., bullying, harassment)

Strategies for Managing Stress during Traumatic Events

1. Prioritize safety and security
2. Seek social support and connection
3. Engage in self-care and relaxation techniques
4. Practice mindfulness and presence
5. Use positive self-talk and affirmations
6. Set boundaries and prioritize self-protection
7. Seek professional help and therapy
8. Engage in activities that promote control and empowerment
9. Practice self-compassion and self-forgiveness
10. Focus on resilience and post-traumatic growth

Additional Tips for Managing Stress during Traumatic Events

1. Allow yourself to feel emotions and process them
2. Take care of physical health and well-being

3. Use creative expression and art therapy
4. Practice gratitude and appreciation
5. Seek out support groups and community
6. Focus on the present moment and what can be controlled
7. Develop a growth mindset and focus on personal growth
8. Engage in activities that promote relaxation and stress reduction
9. Practice self-awareness and self-reflection
10. Celebrate small victories and accomplishments

Understanding the impact of traumatic events on stress levels and implementing effective strategies for managing stress, individuals can navigate these difficult situations with greater resilience and hope for recovery. Remember, traumatic events are not a sign of weakness, and seeking help is a sign of strength.

Part 5: Advanced Stress Management Techniques

Chapter 17: Cognitive-Behavioral Therapy for Stress Management

Cognitive-behavioral therapy (CBT) is a highly effective form of psychotherapy that focuses on the relationship between thoughts, feelings, and behaviors. In the context of stress management, CBT helps individuals identify and challenge negative thought patterns, reframe unhelpful beliefs, and develop coping skills to manage stress. In this chapter, we will explore the principles of CBT, its application to stress management, and provide a comprehensive guide to CBT techniques and strategies.

Principles of Cognitive-Behavioral Therapy

1. **Cognitive-behavioral theory:** Emphasizes the role of thoughts, beliefs, and attitudes in shaping behavior and emotions.
2. **Collaborative approach:** Therapist and client work together to identify and challenge negative thoughts and behaviors.
3. **Present-focused:** Emphasizes current thoughts, feelings, and behaviors rather than past experiences.
4. **Problem-oriented:** Targets specific problems and goals.
5. **Educative:** Teaches clients skills and strategies to manage stress and emotions.
6. **Structured:** Follows a clear and systematic approach.
7. **Time-limited:** Typically involves a limited number of sessions.

Application of CBT to Stress Management

1. **Identifying negative thought patterns:**
Helps clients recognize distorted or
unhelpful thinking.
2. **Challenging negative thoughts:**
Encourages clients to question and reframe
negative beliefs.
3. **Developing coping skills:** Teaches
clients effective coping strategies and
techniques.
4. **Managing stressors:** Helps clients
identify and manage stressors in their
environment.
5. **Building resilience:** Fosters coping skills
and strategies to enhance resilience.

CBT Techniques and Strategies for Stress Management

1. **Cognitive restructuring:** Helps clients
identify and challenge negative thoughts.
2. **Exposure therapy:** Encourages clients
to confront feared situations or stimuli.

3. **Mindfulness-based stress reduction:** Teaches clients mindfulness techniques to manage stress.
4. **Relaxation training:** Helps clients develop relaxation skills to reduce stress.
5. **Problem-solving training:** Teaches clients effective problem-solving skills.
6. **Social support building:** Encourages clients to develop social support networks.
7. **Self-care training:** Teaches clients self-care skills and strategies.
8. **Stress management planning:** Helps clients develop a plan to manage stress.

Additional Tips for CBT and Stress Management

1. Practice self-compassion and self-awareness.
2. Engage in regular relaxation and mindfulness practices.
3. Develop a growth mindset and focus on personal growth.

4. Seek social support and build a support network.
5. Take breaks and engage in activities that bring joy and fulfillment.
6. Focus on the present moment and what can be controlled.
7. Develop a sense of purpose and meaning.
8. Engage in physical activity and exercise regularly.

By having the right knowledge of the principles of CBT and applying its techniques and strategies to stress management, individuals can develop effective coping skills, manage stress, and enhance overall well-being. Remember, CBT is a collaborative and present-focused approach that empowers individuals to take control of their thoughts, feelings, and behaviors.

Chapter 18: Journaling and Reflection for Stress Relief

Journaling and reflection are powerful tools for stress relief, offering a safe and creative outlet for processing emotions, exploring thoughts, and gaining insight. By committing thoughts and feelings to paper, individuals can clarify their experiences, identify patterns and triggers, and develop a greater understanding of themselves. In this chapter, we will explore the benefits of journaling and reflection for stress relief, discuss various journaling techniques, and provide guidance on how to incorporate journaling into daily life.

Benefits of Journaling and Reflection for Stress Relief

1. Emotional release and expression
2. Clarification of thoughts and feelings

3. Identification of patterns and triggers
4. Development of self-awareness and insight
5. Reduction of stress and anxiety
6. Improvement of mental health and well-being
7. Enhanced creativity and problem-solving skills
8. Increased gratitude and positivity
9. Better sleep quality
10. Improved physical health

Journaling Techniques for Stress Relief

1. Stream-of-consciousness writing
2. Prompt-based journaling (e.g., gratitude, goals, emotions)
3. Free writing (e.g., 10-minute timed writing)
4. Reflective journaling (e.g., exploring experiences, thoughts, feelings)
5. Creative journaling (e.g., art, doodles, collages)

6. Mindfulness journaling (e.g.,
present-moment awareness)
7. Self-care journaling (e.g.,
self-compassion, self-forgiveness)
8. Goal-oriented journaling (e.g., setting,
achieving, reflecting)
9. Travel journaling (e.g., documenting
experiences, memories)
10. Digital journaling (e.g., apps, online
platforms)

Incorporating Journaling into Daily Life

1. Schedule journaling time (e.g., morning,
evening, lunch breaks)
2. Choose a comfortable and quiet space
3. Select a journal that suits your style (e.g.,
paper, digital, size)
4. Start small (e.g., 5-10 minutes, 2-3 times
a week)
5. Experiment with different techniques and
prompts
6. Make journaling a habit (e.g., daily,
weekly, consistently)

7. Reflect on your journal entries (e.g., patterns, progress, insights)
8. Use journaling as a tool for self-care and stress relief
9. Be patient and kind to yourself throughout the process
10. Celebrate your growth and progress

Additional Tips for Journaling and Reflection

1. Be honest and authentic in your writing
2. Use journaling as a safe space for expression
3. Explore different journaling styles and techniques
4. Reflect on your experiences and emotions
5. Identify patterns and triggers for stress
6. Develop a growth mindset and focus on personal growth
7. Use journaling as a tool for self-awareness and insight

8. Practice self-compassion and self-forgiveness
9. Celebrate your strengths and accomplishments
10. Embrace the journey of journaling and reflection

By incorporating journaling and reflection into daily life, individuals can cultivate a deeper understanding of themselves, manage stress and emotions, and enhance overall well-being. Remember, journaling is a personal and creative process, and there is no right or wrong way to do it.

Chapter 19: Seeking Professional Help for Stress Management

Seeking professional help is a crucial step in managing stress, especially when it becomes overwhelming and interferes with daily life. Mental health professionals, such as therapists, counselors, and psychologists, offer a safe and supportive environment to explore stressors, develop coping strategies, and improve overall well-being. In this chapter, we will discuss the benefits of seeking professional help, types of professionals who can assist with stress management, and what to expect during therapy.

Benefits of Seeking Professional Help

1. Expert guidance and support
2. Personalized coping strategies
3. Improved stress management skills
4. Enhanced emotional regulation
5. Increased self-awareness and understanding

6. Development of healthy habits and routines
7. Improved relationships and communication skills
8. Increased resilience and stress tolerance
9. Reduced symptoms of anxiety and depression
10. Improved overall mental health and well-being

Seeking professional help for stress management is a crucial step towards achieving a healthier and more balanced life. Here are some ways to seek professional help:

1. **Primary Care Physician:**
   - Start by consulting your primary care physician, who can refer you to a specialist or provide guidance on managing stress.
   - Discuss your stress levels, symptoms, and concerns with your doctor.
2. **Mental Health Professionals:**

- Therapists (e.g., psychotherapists, cognitive-behavioral therapists)
- Counselors (e.g., mental health counselors, marriage and family therapists)
- Psychologists (e.g., clinical psychologists, neuropsychologists)
- Psychiatrists (for medication management)

3. **Online Therapy Platforms:**
- Online therapy platforms like BetterHelp, Talkspace, and 7 Cups offer convenient and accessible therapy sessions with licensed professionals.

4. **Hotlines and Support Services:**
- National Suicide Prevention Lifeline (1-800-273-TALK)
- Crisis Text Line (text HOME to 741741)
- Stress management hotlines and support services offered by health insurance providers or employee assistance programs (EAPs)

5. **Employee Assistance Programs (EAPs):**

- Many companies offer EAPs, which provide confidential counseling services for employees and their families.

6. **Health Insurance Providers:**

   - Check your health insurance provider's website or contact their customer service to find in-network mental health professionals and stress management resources.

7. **Professional Associations:**

   - American Psychological Association (APA)
   - National Association of Social Workers (NASW)
   - American Counseling Association (ACA)

8. **Local Mental Health Clinics:**

   - Community mental health clinics offer affordable and accessible therapy sessions with licensed professionals.

9. **Support Groups:**

   - Join a support group, either in-person or online, to connect with others who are experiencing similar stress and mental health challenges.

10. **Self-Help Resources:**

   - Utilize self-help resources like books, articles, and online stress management tools to supplement professional help.

Remember, seeking professional help is a sign of strength, and there is no shame in asking for support when needed.

Types of Professionals Who Can Assist with Stress Management

1. Therapists (e.g., psychotherapists, cognitive-behavioral therapists)
2. Counselors (e.g., mental health counselors, marriage and family therapists)
3. Psychologists (e.g., clinical psychologists, neuropsychologists)
4. Psychiatrists (for medication management)
5. Social workers (e.g., licensed clinical social workers)
6. Coaches (e.g., life coaches, wellness coaches)

7. Mindfulness and meditation instructors
8. Stress management specialists
9. Holistic health practitioners (e.g., acupuncturists, naturopaths)
10. Online therapists and counselors (for convenience and accessibility)

What to Expect During Therapy

1. Initial consultation and assessment
2. Development of a personalized treatment plan
3. Regular sessions (e.g., weekly, biweekly, monthly)
4. Exploration of stressors and emotions
5. Learning and practicing coping strategies
6. Setting and working towards goals
7. Building self-awareness and understanding
8. Addressing underlying issues and concerns
9. Developing healthy habits and routines
10. Ongoing support and guidance

Preparing for Therapy

1. Identify your stressors and concerns
2. Research and find a qualified professional
3. Schedule an initial consultation
4. Be honest and open about your feelings and experiences
5. Be willing to work collaboratively and actively
6. Set realistic expectations and goals
7. Be patient and kind to yourself throughout the process
8. Take notes and reflect on your progress
9. Celebrate your growth and accomplishments
10. Embrace the journey of therapy and self-improvement

Additional Tips for Seeking Professional Help

1. Don't hesitate to seek help when needed

2. Prioritize your mental health and well-being
3. Be open-minded and receptive to new ideas and strategies
4. Develop a growth mindset and focus on personal growth
5. Practice self-compassion and self-forgiveness
6. Celebrate your strengths and accomplishments
7. Embrace the process of therapy and self-improvement
8. Take care of your physical health and well-being
9. Surround yourself with supportive people and environments
10. Remember that seeking help is a sign of strength, not weakness.

By seeking professional help, individuals can develop the skills and strategies necessary to manage stress effectively, improve their mental health and well-being, and enhance their overall quality of life.

Remember, seeking help is a sign of strength, and there is no shame in asking for support when needed.

Chapter 20:
Creating a Personalized Stress Management Plan

Creating a personalized stress management plan is a crucial step towards achieving a healthier and more balanced life. By understanding individual stressors, goals, and preferences, individuals can develop a tailored plan that effectively manages stress and improves overall well-being. In this chapter, we will explore the importance of personalized stress management, discuss the steps to create a personalized plan, and provide examples and resources to support the process.

Importance of Personalized Stress Management

1. **Effective stress management:** A personalized plan addresses specific stressors and goals, leading to more effective stress management.
2. **Increased motivation:** A tailored plan boosts motivation and engagement, as individuals are more likely to follow a plan that suits their needs.
3. **Improved self-awareness:** The planning process enhances self-awareness, helping individuals understand their stressors, strengths, and weaknesses.
4. **Enhanced resilience:** A personalized plan fosters resilience, enabling individuals to better cope with stress and adversity.

5. **Better time management:** A plan helps individuals prioritize tasks, manage time, and maintain a healthy work-life balance.

Steps to Create a Personalized Stress Management Plan

1. **Identify stressors:** Reflect on personal and professional stressors, including relationships, work, finances, and health.
2. **Set goals:** Establish specific, measurable, achievable, relevant, and time-bound (SMART) goals for stress management and overall well-being.
3. **Assess preferences:** Consider individual preferences, such as relaxation techniques, exercise, or social support.
4. **Develop strategies:** Select effective stress management strategies, including mindfulness, self-care, and time management techniques.
5. **Create an action plan:** Outline specific actions, timelines, and resources needed to implement the plan.

6. **Implement and evaluate:** Put the plan into action, regularly assessing progress and making adjustments as needed.

Examples and Resources

1. Stress management worksheets and templates
2. Mindfulness and relaxation apps (e.g., Headspace, Calm)
3. Physical activity and exercise resources (e.g., fitness classes, walking groups)
4. Social support networks (e.g., support groups, online communities)
5. Time management tools (e.g., planners, productivity apps)
6. Self-care resources (e.g., meditation, yoga, spa services)

Additional Tips

1. **Be patient and flexible:** Adjust the plan as needed to accommodate changing circumstances.

2. **Prioritize self-care:** Make time for activities that bring joy and relaxation.
3. **Seek support:** Share the plan with a trusted friend, family member, or mental health professional.
4. **Celebrate progress:** Acknowledge and celebrate achievements along the way.
5. **Embrace lifelong learning:** Continuously seek new knowledge and skills to enhance stress management and overall well-being.

By creating a personalized stress management plan, individuals can take control of their stress, improve their mental and physical health, and enhance their overall quality of life. Remember, stress management is a journey, and a personalized plan is a powerful tool for achieving success.

Conclusion

Summary of Key Takeaways

This book provides a comprehensive guide to understanding and managing stress. Here is a summary of the key takeaways:

- Stress is a natural response to perceived threats, but chronic stress can have severe physical and mental health consequences.

- Effective stress management requires a holistic approach, incorporating physical, emotional, and mental well-being.

- Identifying and understanding personal stressors is crucial for developing effective coping strategies.

- Relaxation techniques such as deep breathing, progressive muscle relaxation, and visualization can help reduce stress and anxiety.

- Regular physical activity, healthy eating, and sufficient sleep are essential for managing stress and improving overall health.

- Social support from family, friends, and colleagues can play a vital role in stress management.

- Mindfulness practices such as meditation and yoga can help reduce stress and improve mental clarity.

- Cognitive-behavioral therapy (CBT) is a helpful approach for managing stress and anxiety by changing negative thought patterns.

- Journaling and reflection can aid in processing emotions and gaining insight into personal stressors.

- Seeking professional help from mental health professionals, support groups, or hotlines is essential for managing severe stress and mental health concerns.

- Creating a personalized stress management plan that incorporates individual preferences, goals, and strategies is crucial for effective stress management.

- Self-care, time management, and setting boundaries are essential for maintaining a healthy work-life balance and reducing stress.

- Practicing gratitude, self-compassion, and self-awareness can help build resilience and improve overall well-being.

- Effective stress management is a continuous process that requires patience, persistence, and a willingness to learn and adapt.

By applying these key takeaways, individuals can develop effective stress management strategies, improve their overall well-being, and enhance their quality of life. Remember, stress management is a journey, and it's essential to be patient, kind, and compassionate with yourself throughout the process.

Encouragement for Ongoing Stress Management

Congratulations on taking the first step towards managing stress! Recognizing the importance of stress management is a significant accomplishment, and you should be proud of yourself. Remember, stress management is a journey, not a destination. It requires ongoing effort, patience, and self-compassion. Here are some encouraging words to help you continue on this path:

1. Celebrate small victories: Acknowledge and celebrate each small success, even if it seems insignificant. This will help you stay motivated and encouraged throughout the process.

2. Be patient with yourself: Remember that stress management is a process that takes time, effort, and practice. Don't be too hard on yourself if you encounter setbacks or difficulties along the way.

3. Embrace self-care: Prioritize self-care activities, such as exercise, meditation, and spending time with loved ones. These activities will help you recharge and reduce stress.

4. Seek support: Surround yourself with supportive people who encourage and

motivate you. Don't be afraid to ask for help when you need it.

5. Focus on progress, not perfection: Remember that stress management is about progress, not perfection. Focus on the steps you're taking towards a healthier, happier you, rather than dwelling on setbacks.

6. Practice self-compassion: Treat yourself with kindness, understanding, and patience. Remember that everyone experiences stress and setbacks, and it's okay to not be perfect.

7. Embrace mindfulness: Focus on the present moment and let go of worries about the past or future. Mindfulness techniques can help you stay grounded and centered.

8. Take breaks and rest: Allow yourself time to rest and recharge. Taking breaks can

help you come back stronger and more focused.

9. Stay positive: Focus on the positive aspects of your life and express gratitude for what you have. A positive attitude can help you navigate stress and challenges more effectively.

10. Keep learning: Continuously seek new knowledge and skills to enhance your stress management toolkit. This will help you stay motivated and engaged in the process.

11. Embrace challenges: View challenges as opportunities for growth and learning. Remember that every experience, no matter how difficult, can teach you something valuable.

12. Prioritize sleep and nutrition: Adequate sleep and nutrition are essential for managing stress. Make sure to prioritize these aspects of your health.

13. Stay connected: Build and maintain strong relationships with friends, family, and colleagues. Social support is crucial for stress management.

14. Find activities you enjoy: Engage in activities that bring you joy and fulfillment. This can help distract you from stress and improve your overall well-being.

15. Remember, you're not alone: Stress is a common experience that affects everyone. Remember that you're not alone, and there are resources available to support you.

Remember, stress management is a journey that requires ongoing effort and commitment. Stay encouraged, motivated, and patient with yourself as you continue on this path. Celebrate your successes, no matter how small, and don't be afraid to seek help when you need it. You got this!

Appendix

Additional Resources for Stress Management

- **BetterHelp:** An online therapy service that matches you to licensed, accredited therapists who can help with depression, anxiety, relationships, and more.

- **Exercise:** Physical activity is a huge stress reliever, and you don't have to be an athlete or spend hours in a gym to experience the benefits.

- **Face-to-face interaction:** Spending quality time with another human being who makes you feel safe and understood can help you feel more calm.

- **Social Support:** Building and maintaining a network of close friends can improve your resiliency to life's stressors.

- **Stress & Burnout Prevention Exercises:** Science-based exercises will equip you and those you work with tools to manage stress better and find a healthier balance in your life.

- **Workplace Stress Management:** Workplace stress management and wellness programs can help reduce the degree and impact of stress and restore an employee's depleted psychological resources.

- **Workshops:** Workshops can help you understand specific stressors and take positive steps to reduce their effects.

- **WSM Interventions:** WSM interventions are typically divided into three types: primary, secondary and tertiary. Primary is proactive and involved in preventing stress and promoting employee wellbeing, secondary is proactive and reactive, to help remove risk factors, and tertiary is reactive, for employees who need help.

Stress Management Worksheets and Templates

- **Breath Awareness:** This worksheet is designed to help individuals cultivate a mindful awareness of their breathing and the present moment rather than get caught up in their thoughts. It is a breathing exercise that can be useful during moments of distress to unhook someone from their thoughts or as a mindfulness exercise.

- **Anchor Breathing**: This worksheet involves inhaling and exhaling consciously while focusing on the physical experience. In this exercise, clients are also instructed to imagine a peaceful scene – being on a boat, feeling calm and safe. Deep breathing techniques have been shown to lead to decreased oxygen consumption and heightened alertness.

- **The Five Senses Worksheet:** This worksheet cultivates mindfulness by paying attention to what we observe and feel while using our different senses one at a time. During mindfulness practice, distractions are observed, and attention is gently returned to the body part receiving focus.

- **Anxiety Record:** This worksheet helps individuals understand what is causing their anxiety and learn appropriate coping skills. Using this worksheet, clients can record their anxieties, triggers, and their effects.

Afterward, they are guided through a breathing exercise and asked to revisit their answers to the questions.

- **Urge Surfing:** This worksheet is available with a subscription to the Positive Psychology Toolkit©. Backed up by scientific research, mindful self-acceptance can teach individuals to observe their cravings rather than act upon them.

- **Meditation on the Soles of the Feet:** This worksheet provides a safe space to work on managing strong emotions and regulating the urge to be aggressive, often a byproduct of stressful situations. The individual is not asked to stop angry thoughts – anger does serve a useful purpose at times – but rather to bring them under control through a shift of focus.